NERD GUIDE™ SIMPLE FACTORY ARCHITECTURE WITH C#

This work is Nerd Certified™ through *Nerd Guide's* Nerd Certification process.

To learn more about this and our other Nerd Guide publications please visit *http://www.nerdguide.org*.

NERD GUIDE™ SIMPLE FACTORY ARCHITECTURE WITH C#

FIRST EDITION

PUBLISHED BY
Nerd Guide, P.O. Box 15559, Rochester, New York

ISBN-13: 978-1483933504
ISBN-10: 1483933504

*"Believe in yourself because few will do it for you.
Nevertheless, I will be one of those few."*
- Daniel Diaz III©

Preface

The book was written for all those who wanted a download from me on software architecture. This is one "simple" nugget I give to the world. I hope you find it educational, interesting, and useful.

The intended primary audience is software developers who want to learn more about software architecture. My hope is that this kind of material will reach those in the beginning stages of a software development career so they can build up a mastery of these types of concepts.

The secondary audience I hope this material reaches is those already in some architect role. The goal for this group is that they would hang on to this type of material for reference.

The "simple" nugget provided in this book I have seen in the work place and used myself many times over throughout my career. It is a value-add to use in software development or in software design.

Working on this book was a great experience. This one took about two weeks for me to write up and move to final proof. As always, I learned a little more by working on this book. Writing seems to be a great character development process.

A special thank you must be given to all my family and friends who put up with my absence, sanity (or lack of it), ranting, work time, and love.

This one is done, I think its fishing time...

Introduction

Factory based software architecture is a popular creational pattern used today. With it, you can decouple one or more software layers and eliminate the coding burden of object creation. This is done by allowing a factory to create an object without specifying the exact object class. We will explore the Simple Factory model, which is derived from the Factory pattern. Examples are provided later using Visual C#.

Tip: Do an internet search for "creational pattern" and "factory pattern" to learn more.

A Simple Factory will return a single instance of one of several possible class options. The factory will need a reference to the object interface even though the exact concrete class is not required. The main purpose of this Simple Factory design pattern is to separate the object creation process from the current implementation context. In code, use the factory to create objects based on the parameter values passed to it. The factory will then provide each object requested.

We can find a practical implementation of the Simple Factory inside the Microsoft provided Enterprise Library. In the Data Access Application Block of the Enterprise Library there is class named *Database*. This is the base class for the frequently used *SqlDatabase* & *OracleDatabase* classes. The factory class used is called the *DatabaseFactory*. This *DatabaseFactory* class has a method named *CreateDatabase(string name)*. The *CreateDatabase* method allows you to create an instance of type *Database*. This Database type can be a *SqlDatabase* or *OracleDatabase* based on the parameter *name* value sent into the factory. In code, the developer will not care which class instance is returned (*SqlDatabase* or *OracleDatabase*) as long as they all have the same methods.

Tip: Search for "Enterprise Library" or the highlighted class names to learn more.

Take a look at Figure 1 which depicts what happens when the Simple Factory is used. Consider this standard setup with data coming from a user interface (UI) then being sent to the factory that will produce the concrete class to work with. Simple, right? Some real code examples used later on will further explain how this will work. Note that the use of classes in this model is currently considered a legacy implementation.

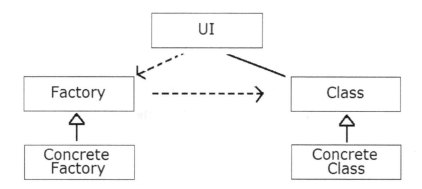

Figure 1. *Simple Factory Process.* Daniel Diaz. 2013.

Why Use a Design Pattern?

The factory pattern is one of many software design options. A software architect should consider using a standard pattern for one of several reasons. Let us explore some of those reasons:

A design pattern is usually based in experience. Using a pattern will take advantage of another's previous learning's. A good pattern will make software more readable. The right pattern will make future design and build initiatives easier through template like design that will be easy for developers and architects to follow. The right design will lead to improved software scalability. Design patterns can reduce the system coupling between classes. This will make the class only dependent on a class implementation, an interface, or abstract class inheritance. The decoupling process removes the necessity of knowledge about any lower class. Good patterns will improve code reuse while popular patterns can provide some common problems with ready-made solutions.

Advantages of the Simple Factory

As mentioned before, object creation can be abstracted thus adding an additional software layer. The object creation of the concrete classes can be controlled through values such as parameters passed to the factory, configuration values stored in a file, or values stored a database. Using the Simple Factory allows you to add new concrete classes and methods later on

6

without breaking the functionality of existing code. Take note of other advantages to this approach:

- Decouple structure from application
- Remove burden of object creation
- Reduce duplication of code
- Eliminate insufficient information problems at object creation time
- Factory methods encapsulate the creation of objects
- Useful to hide objects and methods through abstraction
- Improve software readability
- Make software more scalable

Limitations of the Simple Factory

There are some gotchas to be aware of when the Simple Factory pattern is applied to new or existing code. Here are a few:

- Will require change in one or more existing code layers
- Limits how classes are extend in the future
- Adds some overhead as an extended subclass must provide its own implementation of all factory methods with the same signatures
- The Simple Factory returns only one class instance

When to Use the Simple Factory

Consider use of the Simple Factory pattern when the creation of an object precludes its reuse without significant duplication of code. Make use of this when the creation of an object requires access to stuff that should not be included within the creating class. Also, use the Simple Factory when the lifecycle management of the factory objects must be centralized. All this will ensure consistent behavior and application. This model is best used when getting an object will be a more complex process than simply creating a new object.

Tools for Implementation

There are some popular tools available for those who use factories. These tools can enhance your code. We will not be discussing the details of these however be aware of them:

- Autofac
- Castle Windsor
- LinFu
- Ninject (Titan)
- PicoContainer.NET
- Puzzle.Nfactory
- S2Container.NET
- StructureMap
- Spring.NET
- Unity

Tip: Search for "Dependency Injection" to learn more about what these type tools can do for you.

Simple Factory Explained with Code

Here is code that we would write if we did not use a factory:

```
// code we want to avoid having to work out ...
switch (animalType) {
case"Cat":
    Cat c = new Cat();
        cat.Save(data);
    break;
case "Dog":
        Dog dog = new Dog();
        dog.Save(data);
    break;
case "Fish":
        Fish fish = new Fish();
        fish.Save(data);
    break;
} ...
```

It would be cleaner to be able to express the above like this:

```
// better implementation...
void Save(Animal  animalSelection, object data) {
IAnimal animal = Factory.Animal.Create(animalSelection);
animal.Save(data); } ...
```

Do you like the change? Let's take a look at what we need to do to get there with some example code.

First, we need to make sure each animal has a standard structure. We do this by making an interface that all animals inherit.

```
// Interface to enforce that each animal has a Save method...
// Project.Interface
public interface IAnimal
{
    bool Save(object data);
} ...
```

For good coding pratice let's use an enumator to list our animal options.

```
using System.ComponentModel;

// Our animals
// Project.Constants
public enum Animal {
    [Description("Cat")]
    Cat = 1,
    [Description("Dog")]
    Dog = 2,
    [Description("Fish")]
    Fish = 3
}
```

Next, let's build our animals that will inherit from *IAnimal* and link into a data layer:

```
//Concrete business classes
// Project.Business
public class Cat : IAnimal {
   public bool Save(object data)
   {
      return Project.Data.Save.Cat(data);
   }
}

 public class Dog : IAnimal {
   public bool Save(object data)
   {
      return Project.Data.Save.Dog(data);
   }
}

public class Fish : IAnimal {
   public bool Save(object data)
   {
      return Project.Data.Save.Fish(data);
   }
}
```

Finally, we need a Simple Factory:

```
// Simple Factory
// Project.Business
using Project.Constants;
using Project.Interface;

public static class Animal : IFactory
{
    // variation on classic factory using enum
    public static IAnimal Create(Constants.Animal animal)
    {
        IAnimal value=null;

        switch (animal) {
          case Constants.Animal.Cat:
            value = new Cat();
                break;
          case Constants.Animal.Dog:
            value = new Dog();
                break;
          case Constants.Animal.Fish:
            value = new Fish();
                break;
        }
        return value;
    }
```

```
// classic form of factory using method overload
public static IAnimal Create(string animal)
    {
      IAnimal value=null;

      switch (animal.ToLower()) {
        case "cat":
          value = new Cat();
              break;
        case "dog":
          value = new Dog();
              break;
        case "fish":
          value = new Fish();
              break;
      }
      return value;
    }

} // end of class
```

Next, let us take a look at the *IFactory* interface. We use this incase we build other factories, so that every factory can have a shared base definition.

```
// Project.Interface
using Project.Constants;

public interface IFactory  {
    IAnimal Create(string animal);
    IAnimal Create(Animal animal);
}
```

Now that we have all the pieces we can use this code to exercise our factory assuming that we receive a selected item from our enumertor list of *Animal* or get a *string* variable with the animal type.

```
// some top code level call (ui) ...
using Project.Business;
using Project.Constants;
using Project.Interface;
...
animal = Factory.Animal.Create(animalSelection);
animal.Save(data);
```

Code Environment Setup

Let us get into more detail on how we can implement the examples we see in the Code Examples section with a more hands on approach. Build your example according to your preferences. You can reference Figure 4, to see how I like to build out mine.

Tip: I always start with a Blank Solution in Visual Studio (VS) then add to it each Project as needed. In VS 2008, add New Project > Visual Studio Solutions > Blank Solution. In VS 2010, add New Project > Installed Templates > Other Project Types > Visual Studio Solutions > Blank Solution. Reference Figure 2, for an example of what to look for.

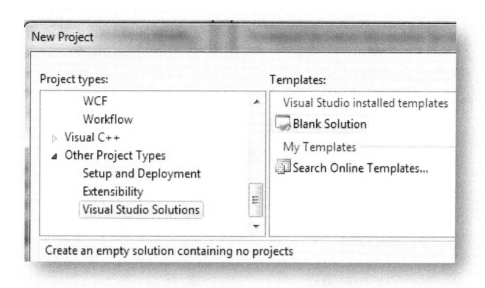

Figure 2. *Visual Studio 2008 Blank Solution.* Daniel Diaz. 2013.

Tip: When I build my Project folder structure I like to build it out like this with the solution file at the top of the file hierarchy:
../Solution File
../ " /Project 1
../ " /Project 2
as seen in Figure 3.

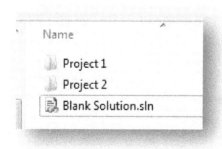

Figure 3. *Folder Structure Example.* Daniel Diaz. 2013.

My project layout is in-line with the code example discussion provided earlier so you can get an idea of how all the pieces we discussed fit together.

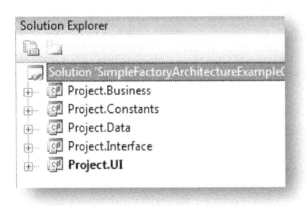

Figure 4. *Project Structure Example.* Daniel Diaz. 2013.

Take note of the code example comments in the previous section. They are there to help indicate which projects the code should be placed in. As part of this section see the provided user interface (UI) code to help you setup a more complete view of this process.

Look at the Windows Form example from Figure 5, which shows that we added a *combobox* called *AnimalList* and a *button* called *Save*.

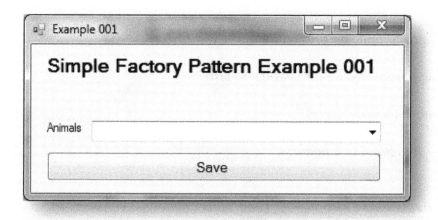

Figure 5. *User Interface Example.* Daniel Diaz. 2013.

Here is our form code, which is held in our first project named *Project.UI*, which a C# Windows Form project. Note, that we have two References 1) *Project Business*, and 2) *Project Constants*:

```
using Project.Business;
using Project.Constants;
using System;
using System.Drawing;
using System.Windows.Forms;
```

```csharp
namespace SimpleFactoryArchitectureExample001
{
  public partial class Example001 : Form
  {
    public Example001()
    {
      InitializeComponent();
    }

    private void Example001_Load(object sender, EventArgs e)
    {
      LoadList();
    }

    private void LoadList()
    {
      AnimalList.DataSource =
      System.Enum.GetValues(typeof(Project.Constants.Animal));
    }

    private void Save_Click(object sender, EventArgs e)
    {
      object someData = new object(); // to represent data to send
      Project.Business.Animal.Save((Project.Constants.Animal)
          AnimalList.SelectedItem, someData);
    }
  }
}
```

The next project layers we see from the UI code are *Project.Constants* and *Project.Business*. We are going to expand upon our previous examples and include a namespace and additional class details. The *Project.Constants* project is a C# Class Library. See Figure 6 for a listing of how

Project.Business was setup. No extra References are required for our *Animal.cs* file:

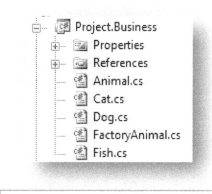

```
using System.ComponentModel;

namespace Project.Constants
{
    public enum Animal
    {
        [Description("Cat")]
        Cat = 1,
        [Description("Dog")]
        Dog = 2,
        [Description("Fish")]
        Fish = 3
    }
}
```

Figure 6. *Project.Business Example.* Daniel Diaz. 2013.

The next collection of files are part of the *Project.Business* C# Class Library which has three extra References: 1) *Project.Constants*, 2) *Project.Data*, and 3) *Project.Interface*. The first class file we will show is called *Animal.cs*:

```
using Project.Constants;
using Project.Interface;
```

19

```
namespace Project.Business
{
    public static class Animal
    {
        public static void Save(Constants.Animal selection, object data)
        {
            IAnimal animal = Factory.Animal.Create(selection);
            animal.Save(data);
        }
    }
}
```

The next file in our *Project.Business* list is called *Cat.cs*:

```
using Project.Data;
using Project.Interface;

namespace Project.Business
{
    public class Cat : IAnimal
    {
        public bool Save(object data)
        {
            return Project.Data.Save.Cat(data);
        }
    }
}
```

The next file is our list is called *Dog.cs*:

```
using Project.Data;
using Project.Interface;

namespace Project.Business
{
   public class Dog : IAnimal
   {
      public bool Save(object data)
      {
         return Project.Data.Save.Dog(data);
      }
   }
}
```

The next file after that is called *Fish.cs,* which I am sure you figured out already what that will look like:

```
using Project.Data;
using Project.Interface;

namespace Project.Business
{
   public class Fish : IAnimal
   {
      public bool Save(object data)
      {
         return Project.Data.Save.Fish(data);
      }
   }
}
```

The final file in our Business collection is called *FactoryAnimal.cs.* This is our Simple Factory:

```
using Project.Business;
using Project.Constants;
using Project.Interface;

namespace Project.Factory
{
  public class Animal
  {
    // variation on classic factory using enum
    public static IAnimal Create(Constants.Animal animal)
    {
      IAnimal value = null;

      switch (animal)
      {
        case Constants.Animal.Cat:
          value = new Cat();
          break;
        case Constants.Animal.Dog:
          value = new Dog();
          break;
        case Constants.Animal.Fish:
          value = new Fish();
          break;
      }
      return value;
    }
```

```csharp
// classic form of factory using method overload
public static IAnimal Create(string animal)
{
    IAnimal value = null;

    switch (animal.ToLower())
    {
        case "cat":
            value = new Cat();
            break;
        case "dog":
            value = new Dog();
            break;
        case "fish":
            value = new Fish();
            break;
    }
    return value;
}

}
}
```

Moving on to the next project which is *Project.Interface* that holds two files as seen in Figure 7. The first file is *IAnimal.cs*:

```csharp
namespace Project.Interface
{
    public interface IAnimal
    {
        bool Save(object data);
    }
}
```

Figure 7. *Project.Interface Example.*
Daniel Diaz. 2013.

23

Then the other file is called *IFactory.cs*:

```
using Project.Constants;

namespace Project.Interface
{
   public interface IFactory  {
      IAnimal Create(string animal);
      IAnimal Create(Animal animal);
   }
}
```

Now the last project in our list is called *Project.Data* that is depicted in Figure 8. Here we are just pretending to do something for the sake of our Simple Architecture exploration. In this project, we have only one file called *Save.cs*:

```
namespace Project.Data
{
   public static class Save
   {
      public static bool Cat(object data) { return true; }
      public static bool Dog(object data) { return true; }
      public static bool Fish(object data) { return true; }
   }
}
```

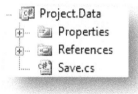

Figure 8. Project.Data Example. Daniel Diaz. 2013.

If you were to implement something real this is where you would replace the *return true;* statements with database or related logic to perform whatever operation you intend to take.

You should now have all the info you need to compile your project then run a working example. Reference Figure 9 to see the UML form of the project we reviewed.

Tip: Build your project in Visual Studio by File Menu > Build > Build Solution. Don't forget to set your Windows Form project as your StartUp Project.

Tip: If you are not familiar with UML diagraming, take time to do some online research looking for "UML Basics".

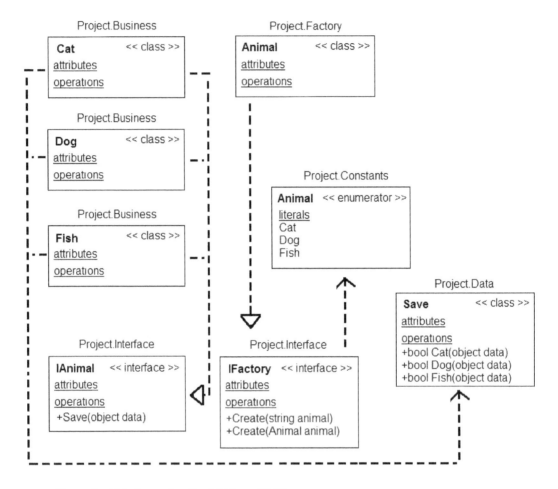

Figure 9. UML Example. Daniel Diaz. 2013.

Other Patterns to Consider

Earlier we discussed why design patterns are good to use. Even though we have focused in on just one, the Simple Factory, be aware of the other options to consider. Reference Tables 1-3 which highlight three main pattern types and the popular methods for each type that get used in software architecture today. The three main patterns categories are: Creational, Structural, and Behavioral. They come out of the 23 Gang of Four (GoF) patterns which are consider the foundation to all other patterns. You may find other Nerd Guide materials that address these other patterns.

Table 1 Creational Patterns	
Abstract Factory	Creates an instance of several families of classes
Builder	Separates object construction from its representation
Factory Method	Creates an instance of several derived classes
Prototype	A fully initialized instance to be copied or cloned
Singleton	A class of which only a single instance can exist

Source: dofactory: .NET Design Patterns
http://www.dofactory.com/Patterns/Patterns.aspx. 03/19/2013.

A Creational Pattern as seen in Table 1 is all about creating objects. Keep in mind that our review of Simple Factory Architecture is not considered an official model it is a practically used process and as such we have included it in our education process. Nevertheless, as we look at Table 2, we see that a Structural Pattern is about establishing relationships between entities.

Table 2 Structural Patterns	
Adapter	Match interfaces of different classes
Bridge	Separates an object's interface from its implementation
Composite	A tree structure of simple and composite objects
Decorator	Add responsibilities to objects dynamically
Façade	A single class that represents an entire subsystem
Flyweight	A fine-grained instance used for efficient sharing
Proxy	An object representing another object

Source: dofactory: .NET Design Patterns
http://www.dofactory.com/Patterns/Patterns.aspx. 03/19/2013.

As we look at Table 3, we see that a Behavioral Pattern is focused on communication between objects. This category has the most patterns to explore.

Tip: To gain a stronger overview of some of the architectural patterns look for other Nerd Guide materials or search online for each pattern to see how others use these structures.

Table 3 Behavioral Patterns	
Chain of Responsibility	A way of passing a request between a chain of objects
Command	Encapsulate a command request as an object
Interpreter	A way to include language elements in a program
Iterator	Sequentially access the elements of a collection
Mediator	Defines simplified communication between classes
Memento	Capture and restore an object's internal state
Observer	A way of notifying change to a number of classes
State	Alter an object's behavior when its state changes
Strategy	Encapsulates an algorithm inside a class
Template Method	Defer the exact steps of an algorithm to a subclass
Visitor	Defines a new operation to a class without change

Source: dofactory: .NET Design Patterns
http://www.dofactory.com/Patterns/Patterns.aspx. 03/19/2013.

Areas of Practical Use

What we have reviewed is some ways the author has seen this Simple Factory pattern practically used in enterprise environments. First of all, many organizations do make use of one of the tools (Unity, Spring, Castle Windsor etc.) mentioned before in conjunction with this pattern. In addition, the use usually is implemented in connection with some legacy code upgrade plan.

One place the Simple Factory gets used a lot is when there is a need for switching between an old class and a new class. Usually the old class is written in a legacy code base or on a different code platform that the software architect is moving away from.

Another way the Simple Factory is implemented frequently is when a whole portion of code like a product module is getting moved from one code platform to another. The Simple Factory is a great way to add a vehicle to easily move processing from the old platform to the new one. A great example of this is for those moving from a Com based architecture to a service based one like with the SOA movement.

Conclusion

Now that you have made it through the definition and description of what a Simple Factory is, hopefully, you can find the right place to use it in your coding endeavors. The practical use discussion should give you some insight as to places you can explore to get this architectural pattern implemented.

Read More

If you found this read above your pay grade, feel free to check out other Nerd Guide works that will help you get closer to this level. Here is a recommended read:

Nerd Guide for Coding C#: Event Driven Programming

ISBN: 780988717640 (paperback)
ISBN: 9780988717626 (ebook)

This is a guide for those who are either beginner or intermediate in programming skill. The book is written with the assumption one already has some programming experience and is now looking to learn more about C#/CSharp. It covers software development using Visual C# for Windows Development and Web Development (ASP.NET). Development environment instructions are provided using Visual Studio. The book provides references to most of the popular applications of the C# language. Most of the basic computers & technology programming concepts are handled by simplified quick reference examples. This material is a condensed and concise learning experience.

About the Author

Globally recognized leader and executive, Daniel Diaz III© is an expert in the high tech industry operating under his specialty of B2B software. He is also an expert technologist and a recognized Nerd. He is officially Nerd Guide's first Nerd Certified™ candidate. Some will recognize him as "TheTechExpert"™. Now he is an author for and founder of Nerd Guide™. Mr. Diaz holds over seventeen years of workforce experience.

His academic credentials include an undergraduate degree in Computer Science and a master's degree in Management. Add to that his industry experience which includes the aerospace, defense, software, finance, and high tech manufacturing sectors. His technology output is influenced by his holistic and analytical view of business, and his conservative investment strategies for maintaining positive cash flow. He is a real finance Nerd.

Mr. Diaz's technical competencies include proficiency with commonly used object oriented program languages such as C#, VB.Net and Java; and expertise with frequently used database systems like MySQL, Oracle RDBMS, and Microsoft SQL Server.

Throughout his career, Mr. Diaz has worked with public, private, non-profit, education, government, and military entities. He holds working knowledge of compliance and certification processes including banking regulation, CMMI, HIPPA, ITIL, and SOX. A summary of his talents includes:

- Executive Leader
- Architect
- Strategist
- Visionary
- Investor
- Fellow Nerd

As a part-time initiative, Mr. Diaz enjoys perpetuating technical education through the Nerd Guide project.

"When normal is not working for you, engage someone who is extraordinary."

About the Publisher

Nerd Guide is the premier publication and education source, providing technical knowledge, concepts, training, and documentation for Nerds. We hope to become a strong non-profit educational source for high tech learning. We look forward to providing materials for all ages.

We are looking for authors (aka Nerds), publishers, translators, bookstores, and other distribution outlets to help us perpetuate these great educational opportunities.

Is high tech education for all your passion? We except donations:

Nerd Guide
P.O. Box 15559
Rochester, New York

Yes, we are not a non-profit yet but that just means you cannot claim your donation as tax deductible. Be patient with us, we will get there, after all we just launched in 2012!

About Nerd Certification

Nerd Guide is continuing to develop its Nerd Certified™ program. Through this initiative, Nerd Guide hopes to provide a platform for Nerds to be certified and credentialed as an official Nerd. In addition to certifying Nerds, we hope to certify products as Nerd worthy through our developing Nerd network. We hope that as this network progresses you who are worthy of being called a Nerd will be willing to participate.

More information about this program will be provided on the website, found at nerdguide.org.

Nerd Guide Branding

To help boost our branding efforts Nerd Guide would like to connect with vendors who can help sell branded Nerd Certified™ and Nerd Guide™ merchandise. Visit our website to see products that are currently available.

Nerd Guide designed this fun, lighthearted program to grow revenues in order to support continued and expanded tech education for all ages.

www.ingramcontent.com/pod-product-compliance
Lightning Source LLC
Chambersburg PA
CBHW060513060326
40689CB00020B/4722